Contents

A
Tl
Pɩ
W
The Vice Commodore, Bert Taylor, of
North Lincs and Humberside Sailing Club
for their advice and use of their facilities.

Photographs on front and back cover and
inside front and back cover courtesy of
Yachting Photographics.

Note Throughout the book dinghy sailors are referred to individually as 'he'. This should, of course, be taken to mean 'he or she' where appropriate.

Introduction

There are thousands of different dinghies that can be sailed; a ship's lifeboat, a tiny fishing boat, a small yacht tender, and so on. Every country has areas where local conditions have encouraged specialist designs, and regattas for many traditional small craft are a popular feature of the sport. Since the fifties the traditionally built, general purpose dinghy has given way to the modern craft, made of light modern materials and designed to be sailed by amateurs just for fun. There has been a revolution in constructional techniques allowing the amateur builder, without any particular skill or training, to build a dinghy at home. Modern dinghies also come in all sizes and shapes, and there are hundreds to choose from.

No matter how old the design, or modern the materials, no matter how long or short, all dinghies are sailed in the same way. Once you have learnt to sail the choice is yours.

What to wear

Unlike the early working dinghies the modern dinghy is virtually unsinkable. The dinghy sailor does not have to be a strong or stylish swimmer, but he should be water-confident, warm and dry while sailing and buoyant if accidentally cast into the water.

Keeping warm means selecting the right clothing, which should be light, warm and comfortable. A pair of light waterproof trousers and a wind and waterproof top covering should help to keep the sailor both warm and dry. To increase buoyancy, a buoyancy aid or life-jacket is worn, and to keep feet and boat from being damaged a pair of light canvas shoes with soft soles are best.

If you intend sailing during early spring, autumn or even winter then more specialised clothing is necessary. This is particularly so if you intend sailing in exposed conditions, high winds, or in a low-profile, and hence very wet, dinghy. Water temperature from mid-autumn until late spring is very cold, particularly in large inland lakes, and

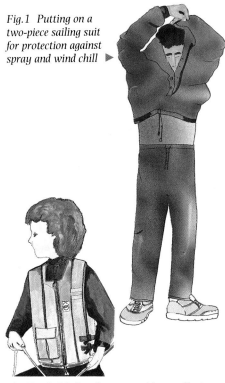

Fig.1 Putting on a two-piece sailing suit for protection against spray and wind chill ▶

▲ *Fig. 2 Modern buoyancy aids are effective and comfortable. Life-jackets are designed to float the wearer face up if unconscious, but are rather cumbersome in small dinghies*

long immersion without appropriate clothing is very dangerous. Luckily, the wonder material neoprene has been available for a very long time now, and modern neoprene suits (or wetsuits) are both comfortable and fashionable. They work by trapping a layer of water inside the suit; this water is then warmed by body heat and so insulates the wearer against further heat loss. The simplest and cheapest suits let in a great deal of water and the initial shock in very cold weather is startling. However, the water soon warms and the sailor is comfortable again. The cheaper suits are not so good if the sailor is involved in several capsizes, because each capsize flushes out the warm water and recharges the suit with cold. More advanced, and expensive, suits are stitched, zipped and sealed at the neck, wrists and ankles to minimise water entry, so several immersions are not a problem. The ultimate protection is given by a dry-suit under which warm clothing is worn. The suits can be rather bulky, but keeping dry is a big advantage.

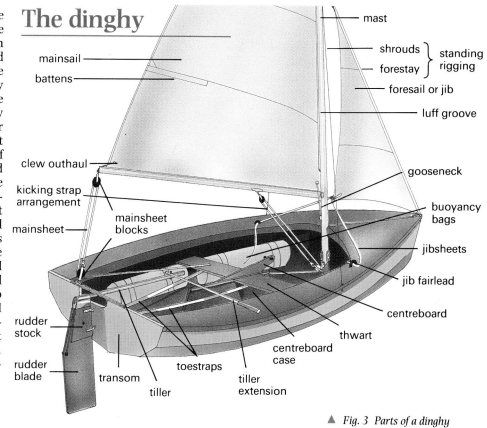

The dinghy

mast

mainsail

battens

shrouds · forestay — standing rigging

foresail or jib

luff groove

clew outhaul

kicking strap arrangement

mainsheet

mainsheet blocks

gooseneck

buoyancy bags

jibsheets

jib fairlead

centreboard

rudder stock

thwart

rudder blade

transom

tiller

toestraps

tiller extension

centreboard case

▲ Fig. 3 Parts of a dinghy

3

The dinghy itself is quite a simple construction. It will have blow-up bags or watertight compartments to make it virtually unsinkable. It will have a mast and boom to carry the sails and a rudder and tiller arrangement so that it can be

▲ *Fig. 4 Raising the mainsail up a luff groove*

▲ *Fig. 5 The sleeved sail of the Topper*

▲ *Fig. 6 Part lacing on a gaff-rigged dinghy*

steered. The dinghy will also have a pivoting centre plate or lift-out daggerboard to prevent it from drifting sideways when sailing across the wind. To hold things together, and to control the sails, there are a variety of pieces of string and rope – 'stays' to hold up the mast and 'sheets' to pull in the sails.

The sail is held by the mast and boom. The front of the sail can be threaded up a slot in the mast, sleeved or simply tied. Sometimes the mast is a single piece; it can be shorter, with a second piece to increase its effective length. This makes very little difference once the sail is set, but it does allow the pieces, or spars, to be stowed inside the dinghy when they are not in use.

Finally, to haul the sails up there are the halyards, one for the front sail and one for the mainsail.

How a dinghy sails

It is easy to understand that a dinghy can be blown with the wind, but less easy to grasp the fact that a dinghy can make progress towards the wind. The triangular mainsail, which most

Beating · Dinghy slows and stops · **THE NO GO ZONE** · Dinghy slows and stops · Beating

The sail no longer sets

Close reaching

Close reaching

Beam reaching

Beam reaching

Fig. 7 The 'no go' zone ▶

5

dinghies carry, allows progress to be made in almost any direction. This is because the sail acts not by being 'pushed' but by allowing the wind to flow across it, creating lift and acting rather like the wing of an aeroplane.

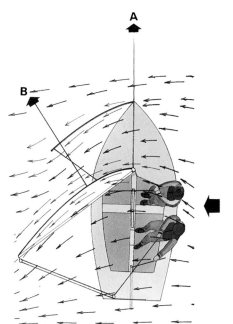

This is possible because when a sail is placed in a stream of air at an angle of about 40° it generates sideways and forwards forces. The sideways forces are cancelled out by the underwater shape of the boat and the centreboard, leaving the forward force to drive the boat along.

When sailing towards the wind, if the sails are pulled in tightly along the centreline of the dinghy, it is possible to sail at about 45° to the wind.

◀ *Fig. 8 The diagram shows the wind flowing across both surfaces of each sail. The sails are pulled in (not too tightly) to maintain a smooth and continuous flow of air over them. The absorbed energy tries to push the dinghies in direction B, but the centreboard prevents sideways movement and the dinghy sails towards A*

Wind and weather

Since it will be driving our dinghy, it is well worth studying the wind in its own right. We all know the effects of the wind on land: it can be gentle or wild, warm or cold and may blow from any direction. A gentle breeze is best for learning – a breeze that can be felt without discomfort and that causes flags and sails to flutter. Modern weather forecasting is now remarkably accurate, and warnings of high winds and blustery weather are fairly reliable. National and local weather forecasts from radio and television are worth listening to. Bands of low pressure crossing the country signify windy weather, as do closely packed isobars on the synoptic charts. Look for a forecast of stable conditions where a gentle breeze is likely, then establish the direction from which it is blowing so that you can plan your sailing accordingly. Be patient: a little caution will help you to get the best out of your first sail. Windspeed and conditions are described by the Beaufort Scale (opposite).

Beaufort scale

Beaufort scale number	Description of wind	Effects of wind on land	Speed in knots
0	Calm	Smoke rises vertically	Less than 1
1	Light air	Smoke drifts, wind vanes do not move	1–3
2	Light breeze	Wind felt on face, leaves rustle, wind vane moves	4–6
3	Gentle breeze	Leaves and twigs move constantly, flags begin to move	7–10
4	Moderate breeze	Raises dust and blows paper along	11–16
5	Fresh breeze	Small trees sway, crested wavelets form on sheltered waters	17–21
6	Strong breeze	Large branches move, telephone lines whistle	22–27
7	Moderate gale	Whole trees move, hard to walk against the wind	28–33
8	Fresh gale	Breaks twigs off trees	34–40
9	Strong gale	Roof slates move, slight structural damage likely	41–47

▲ *Fair weather cumulus clouds*

Beaufort scale number	Description of wind	Effects of wind on land	Speed in knots
10	Whole gale	Trees uprooted, considerable structural damage	48–55
11	Storm	Widespread structural damage	56–65
12	Hurricane	Widespread devastation	Over 65

Launching

A dinghy is light and responsive when on the water, but on land its bulk and weight make it difficult to manage unless it is kept on a launching trolley. This allows the dinghy to be manoeuvred on land by two people with comparative ease. The boat can also be wheeled into the water and floated off the trolley. While the boat is on the trailer, and before it is launched, everything can be made ready. The front sail can be hoisted and the mainsail

▲ *Launching an Enterprise dinghy*

▲ *An extra pair of hands are necessary on a steep slipway*

attached to the boom ready for hoisting. Check to make sure that nothing has been left behind ashore. Most dinghies have drainage holes at the back so that the inside can be drained ashore and rainwater does not stand in the bottom. Before launching make sure that the bungs are securely in place and that the launching trolley is left safely, well above the high-water mark where it won't cause an obstruction.

The dinghy has a piece of rope attached to the front called the painter, which will be secured to the trailer until the dinghy is afloat. The boat is wheeled backwards down the slipway until it

▲ *The trolley is pushed into the water . . .*

▲ *. . . and the dinghy floated off*

floats clear, then the crew holds the dinghy while the helmsman pulls the launching trolley out of the way. If the crew holds the dinghy by the painter it will swing until it is pointing towards the wind.

Reefing

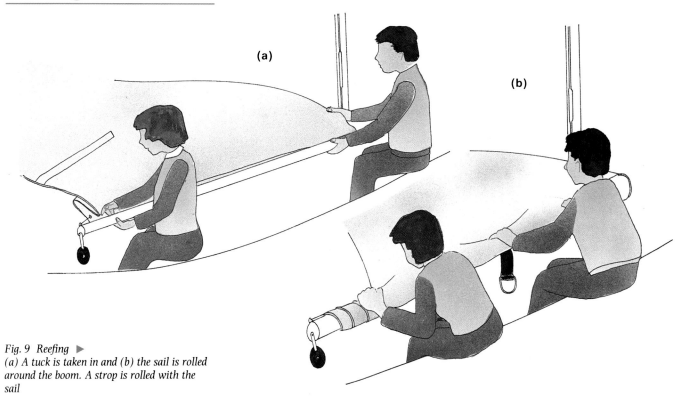

Fig. 9 Reefing ▶
(a) A tuck is taken in and (b) the sail is rolled around the boom. A strop is rolled with the sail

▲ *Enough of it is left out to attach the kicking strap*

▲ *The sail is rolled around the boom to reduce its total area*

Generally only one suit of sails is supplied with a dinghy, and every dinghy in that class has sails with the same sail area. If it is very windy the sails may prove too powerful to handle comfortably and it may be wise to lessen their total area. This is achieved by reefing. The area of the mainsail is reduced by tying in a series of folds (slab reefing) or rolling part of the mainsail around the boom (roller reefing). On some single-handers the sail area can be reduced by rolling part of the mainsail around the mast. It is better to reef your sails before going afloat if you think that the wind strength is likely to increase. If you have practised reefing ashore then reefing afloat should not prove difficult should the need arise. Once you have decided whether or not to reef, the sails can be raised.

◄ *The dinghy crew have hoisted a well-reefed mainsail*

Hoisting the sails

Usually, before the sails are hoisted the rudder is attached and the tiller and extension fixed in place.

Most sails are built in such a way that the third edge (the leech) needs support from battens held in pockets placed at right angles to that edge. Before the sail is hoisted the battens must be inserted. The main halyard is attached to the head of the sail, and the front edge is fed to the slot in the mast as the sail is raised. It is important to raise the sail to the top of the mast, despite the fact that this causes the boom to be lifted above its point of attachment to the mast (the gooseneck).

Once the sail is raised and tied off, the boom can be pulled down and attached – there will be plenty of stretch in the front of the sail to allow this to happen. The boom is kept down by a pulley system called a vang or kicking-strap. This device prevents the boom from lifting as the wind fills the sails. The ends of the halyards are cleated off and coiled tidily. Do not let the halyards fall in a

When the sails are up they will flap in the wind. Do not attempt to hold the boom or the ropes: just let the sails flap until you are ready to sail, and keep your head well out of the way.

▲ *The crew is holding the front of the dinghy allowing it to swing away from the wind. The front sail is hoisted and tied off.*

The foot of the mainsail may be loose, i.e. tied at each end of the boom only, or threaded along a slot in the boom. A pin holds the sails at the mast end and the foot of the sail is pulled taut by a rope through a pulley at the other end

▲ *Fig. 10 The halyards are pulled tight and taken twice around the cleat. A half-hitch is tied on the lower arm of the cleat and the remaining rope coiled*

tangle because you may have to pull your sails down in a hurry.

The first sail

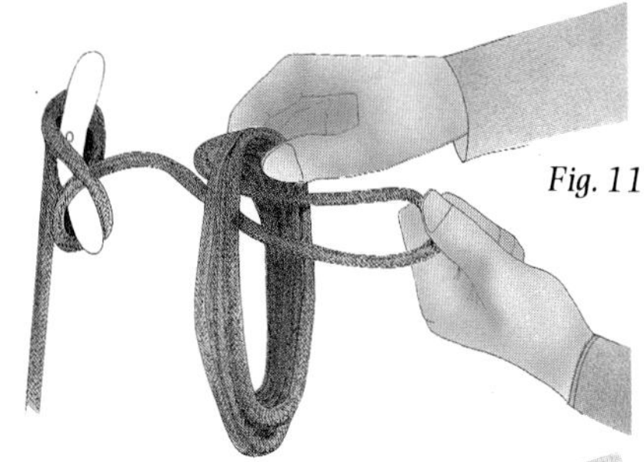

Fig. 11

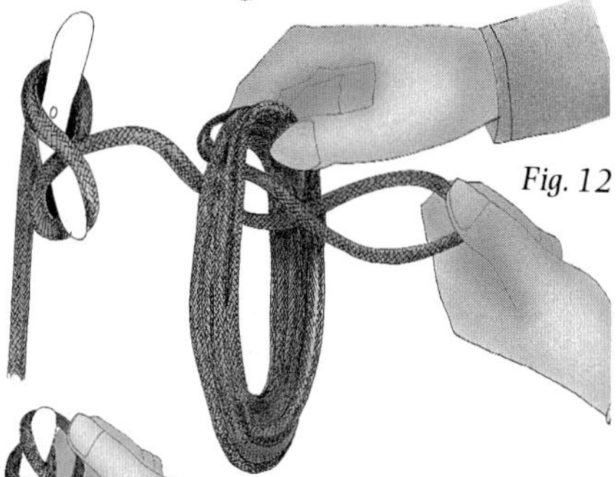

Fig. 12

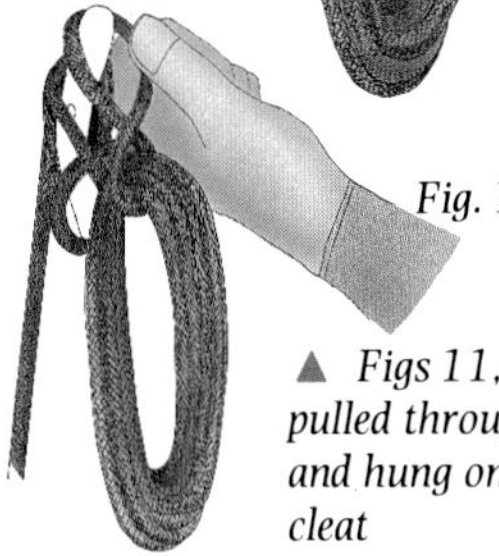

Fig. 13

▲ *Figs 11, 12 and 13 A loop is pulled through the coils, twisted and hung on the top arm of the cleat*

Initially the dinghy will be sailed across the wind, i.e. with the wind blowing from one side of the dinghy to the other. This will allow you to sail away from and return to your starting position without too much difficulty. Winds should be light, and you should choose an inland location or a well-supervised coastal spot used by other dinghy sailors. Better still, sail at a recognised school or at a sailing club where you can get advice and help if needed.

While the crew holds the front of the dinghy, the helmsman makes ready to sail. Usually the water near the beach is too shallow to allow the rudder to go all the way down, so this will have to be pulled to its proper position once the dinghy is away from the beach and in deeper water. The centreboard will have to be pushed halfway down as well, otherwise the dinghy will slip sideways when the sails fill.

The crew pushes the dinghy away until it is lying sideways to the wind, then the helmsman pulls in the mainsail a little as the crew climbs in. While the rudder is being sorted out the crew can push down the centreboard. With helmsman and crew sitting towards the centre of the dinghy on the weather side (the side from which the wind is blowing), the sails are pulled in until they stop flapping and the dinghy is sailing.

Gentle movements of the tiller will establish its effect. The secret is to look forward as the tiller is moved to see how the front of the boat responds. Gentle alterations in course will help, but try not to wander too far from the course that you have set – a course at right angles to the wind.

The speed of the dinghy depends on the set of the sails. If you let the sails right out they will flap and the boat will slow down, perhaps even stop. When you pull them in again, until they *just* stop flapping, the dinghy will pick up speed.

Figs 14 and 15 Sailing across the wind ▶

13

Turning the dinghy (tacking)

Once you have sailed successfully away from your starting point, the dinghy has to be turned around so that you can sail back. The dinghy will turn through 180° so that it is facing the opposite way. It will only turn if it is moving, so keep the sails pulling as you prepare to turn.

You will need to warn your crew and look around to be sure that the way is clear. When everyone is ready, the helmsman changes hands so that he is holding the tiller in his 'front' hand and the rope that controls the mainsail (the main sheet) in his 'back' hand. The tiller is then pushed right across the boat and the helmsman moves slowly under the boom to the other side. As he moves across, he swings the tiller extension right outside the dinghy and then sits down. As the sail fills, he centres the rudder.

During this manoeuvre the crew releases the jib as the dinghy begins to turn, moves with the helmsman across the dingy, and when seated on the other side pulls in the rope which controls the front sail (the jib sheet).

Try this manoeuvre lots of times, remembering to change hands before you move. Above all, try not to rush. Only centre your tiller when your dinghy is pointing in the right direction and the sails have filled again.

Fig. 16 Tacking ▶

14

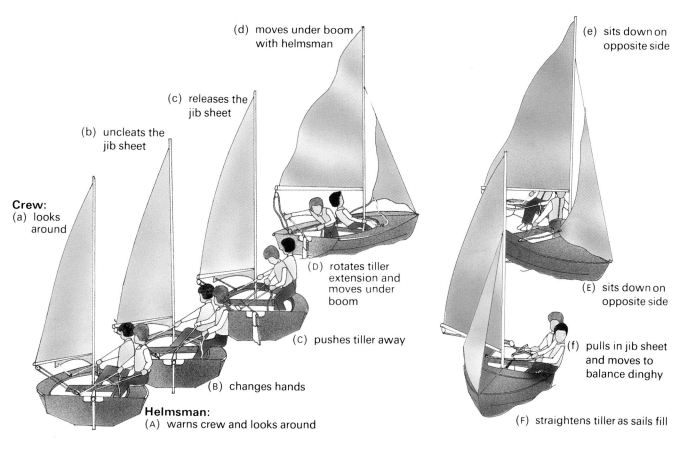

(d) moves under boom with helmsman

(e) sits down on opposite side

(c) releases the jib sheet

(b) uncleats the jib sheet

Crew:
(a) looks around

(D) rotates tiller extension and moves under boom

(E) sits down on opposite side

(C) pushes tiller away

(f) pulls in jib sheet and moves to balance dinghy

(B) changes hands

Helmsman:
(A) warns crew and looks around

(F) straightens tiller as sails fill

Tacking: mainsheet led from centre of boom and hull

▼ *Fig. 17 Tacking*

Many sailing dinghies do not have their mainsheet blocks fitted to the transom and boom end: they have centre mains. Tacking is a little different because throughout the manoeuvre you face forwards. The sequence is as follows (fig. 17(a)–(g)):

● The tiller extension is held in the 'back' hand using a 'dagger' grip. The mainsheet is held in the 'front' hand using the same 'dagger' grip.
● Having looked around you, push the tiller away *without* changing hands.

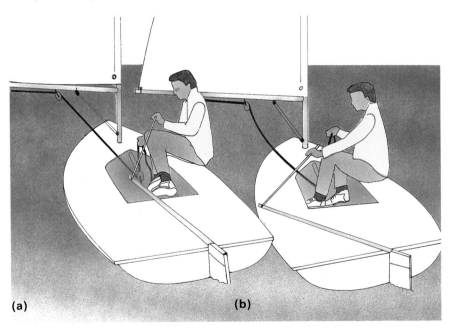

(a)

(b)

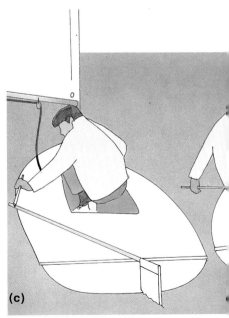

(c)

- You then move under the boom and rotate the tiller extension away from the centre of the dinghy.
- Now sit down, steering from behind. (This may take a little getting used to but persevere!)

- Your back hand, which is still holding the mainsheet, is brought across the front of your body to pick up the tiller extension, while your front hand grasps the mainsheet.

- The tiller extension is then brought back in front of your body, still using the 'dagger' grip.
- Sail away on your new tack.

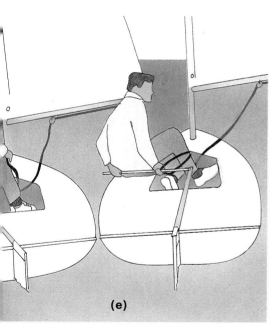

(e)

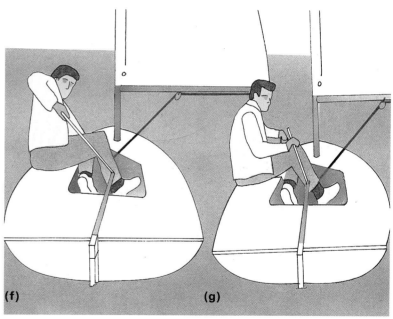

(f) (g)

Sailing above and below your course

When you can turn your dinghy successfully, practise sailing slightly above and below your course. Don't stray too far yet. As you move towards the wind your sails will begin to flap; simply pull them in a little tighter. As you steer away from your new course let your sails out again to their original position. If you let them out too far they will start to flap – just pull them in again until they set without flapping.

As you gain confidence you can venture a little further from your original course, always returning and altering your sail setting as necessary (fig. 18).

▲ *Fig. 18 Sailing above and below your course*

18

Beating

Sailing towards the wind is called beating. When beating, the sideways force on the dinghy is greater than at any other point during sailing. To counteract this, make sure that your centreboard is pushed all the way down. As you bring your dinghy towards the wind the sails will flap and will need to be pulled in a little more each time.

You can go on steering closer to the wind and pulling in the sails until they cannot be pulled any tighter. This is about as far – or as near to the wind – as you can go. If you steer too close to the wind your sails will flap and the dinghy will slow down and eventually stop. Before you reach this point, just steer slightly away from the wind until the sails are set again and the dinghy is moving steadily. When sailing so close to the wind it is a good idea to watch the jib as an indicator of whether or not you have turned too close.

When you are sailing towards the wind or 'close hauled' the dinghy will heel over. To balance your craft,

▲ *Fig. 19 Bringing your dinghy closer to the wind*

helmsman and crew must sit on the side and lean out – don't forget to place your feet under the toe straps just in case ! If your combined weight is not sufficient to balance the dinghy then let out some of the mainsail to reduce the power.

You can now sail towards an upward point. Not directly, of course, but in a series of zig-zags. When you turn your dinghy from a zig to a zag it will only have to turn through 90°, so you will have to centre your tiller *as* you sit down in order to keep on course.

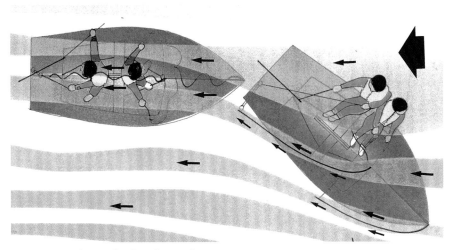

▲ *Fig. 20 Tacking and sailing close to the wind on the opposite tack*

Fig. 21 Sailing across and towards the wind ▶

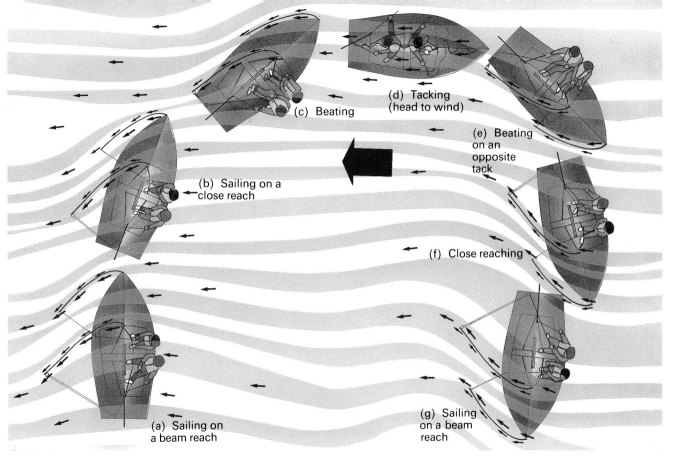

(c) Beating

(d) Tacking (head to wind)

(e) Beating on an opposite tack

(b) Sailing on a close reach

(f) Close reaching

(a) Sailing on a beam reach

(g) Sailing on a beam reach

Sailing away from the wind

When sailing *away* from the wind your sails will be let further and further out (remember if you let them out too far they will flap and you will need to pull them back in again). Practise sailing away from your original starting course away from the wind. Watch your sails carefully. If you sail so far away from the wind that the wind is directly behind the boat, the jib will be blanketed and will collapse. Push the tiller *away* from you a little and the jib will begin to flutter. If you have set your boat correctly before the wind you will feel it blowing across the nearest back corner of the dinghy. When sailing away from the wind you will need less and less of your centreboard in the water because the wind is behind you and not able to blow you sideways.

You can 'run' before the wind with the sails on either side, but it is better always to sail with the jib just catching and not with the wind directly behind you. If you do run dead before the wind, a slight change in the wind's direction could lift sail and boom from one side of the dinghy to the other. This is quite startling when you are not expecting it!

Time practising downwind sailing is very worth while, since it involves making a number of alterations to sails, centreboard and crew positions. Start and finish your practice sessions sailing across the wind (sailing on a beam reach); then bear away, sailing away from the wind. As you steer away from the wind the sideways pressure on the sails is reduced and you will need less centreboard area in the water, so the centreboard can be raised about halfway.

Your crew may not be required to help balance the dinghy, so he or she should move inboard and sit on the thwart. During this time the sails are let out further and further. If they start to flap, pull them in a little – you have probably let them out a bit too far. Carry on sailing away from the wind until the jib begins to be blanketed by the mainsail. When this happens, push the tiller away from you a little and the dinghy is running.

Your next task is to reverse the process by slowly bringing your dinghy back to an across-the-wind course, moving your crew weight and adjusting your centreboard and sails until you are back on your original reaching course.
- The wind is blowing across the stern of the dinghy, the jib is blanketed and collapses.
- The helmsman has brought the jib across the boat so that it is now in the airstream. The crew is holding the boom out in case it should come across if the wind direction changes.
- The helmsman has pushed the tiller away a little, the wind is coming across the dinghy's back corner and the jib is pulling again. This is often a more comfortable way of running.

Notice that the helmsman and crew are no longer sitting together on the same side but have moved apart to balance the dingy.

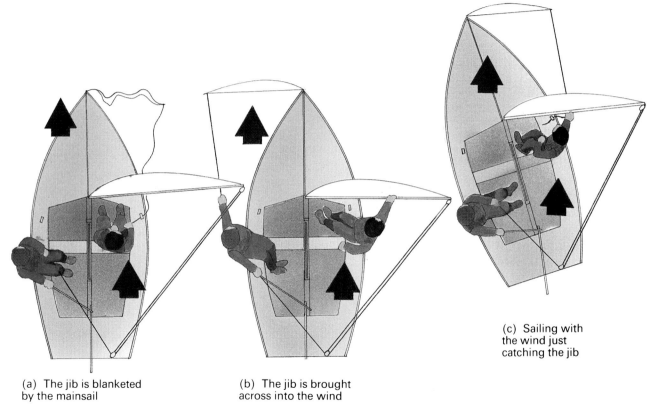

(a) The jib is blanketed by the mainsail

(b) The jib is brought across into the wind

(c) Sailing with the wind just catching the jib

Gybing

When the boat is turned in such a way that the sail will be blown across the centre of the dinghy from one side to the other, the manoeuvre is called *gybing*. To change course by gybing, first check that you are running with the wind just lifting the jib and blowing across the nearest back corner of the dinghy (fig. 23). Check to make sure that if you do alter course you will not run into anyone else. Also warn your crew to be ready.

The sequence is quite straight-forward.

● First change hands, the front hand taking up the tiller extension and the back hand holding the mainsheet.
● Move to place yourself across the centreline of the dinghy facing backwards. As you do this, rotate the tiller extension around and away from you.
● Keep an eye on the boom and then push the tiller over towards where you were sitting.
● As the boat turns, the wind will get

behind the sail and the boom will start to come across.
● As soon as the boom lifts, keep your head down and centre the tiller.
● Once the boom has settled down, sit on your new side and check your course.

▲ *The helmsman has changed hands and is ready to gybe. He is keeping a close eye on the boom!*

▲ *The helmsman straightens the tiller as the boom comes across*

(a) Sailing on a run

(b) Change hands and move to the centre of the dinghy; push down the tiller to where you were sitting

(c) As the boom comes across, centre the tiller

(d) Sit down on the new side

▲ *Fig. 23 Gybing*

If you are sailing a dinghy with a centre mainsheet (*see* photographs), keep the tiller extension in your back hand and swivel it round to the new side as you stand up. Push the tiller over towards where you were sitting and, as the boom comes across, centre the tiller and sit down. As with tacking, steer for a while with the tiller behind you and once on course change hands as you did when tacking (*see* figs 20 and 21).

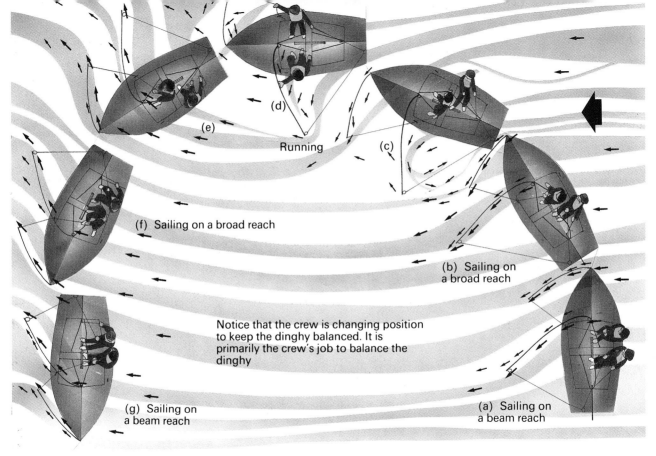

(d)

(e)

Running

(c)

(f) Sailing on a broad reach

(b) Sailing on
a broad reach

Notice that the crew is changing position
to keep the dinghy balanced. It is
primarily the crew's job to balance the
dinghy

(g) Sailing on
a beam reach

(a) Sailing on
a beam reach

▲ Fig. 24 Sailing across and away from the wind

The five essentials

If you are able to tack and gybe successfully then it is time to consider ways and means of sailing your dinghy more efficiently. The wind provides the power, while the weight of the dinghy and crew, and the friction between the hull and the water, resist that power. There will always be some loss of effort and the task will be to minimise the loss. There are five essential areas that need to be considered if you are to get the best possible performance from your dinghy.

Sail-setting

Sails generate power from the wind as it flows across both sides of them. The sailmaker has built your sails using all the scientific knowledge available to him, tempered by his own experience and perception. Modern sails are beautifully made and will often set with hardly a crease, giving a clean smooth profile.

If the sails are pulled in just beyond the position where they begin to flap, the air flow will be smooth and efficient. If the sails are pulled in too tightly, the air will not flow evenly and power will be lost. Because the wind direction is constantly changing, it is important that the helmsman and crew adjust their sails accordingly, letting them out and then pulling them in again until they just set. If you study fig. 24 (*Sailing across and away from the wind*), you will see that the air flows smoothly across the sails. You will also notice that the sails remain in the same position, relative to the wind, on each point of sailing. Look too at the distance between the corner of each dinghy and the end of the boom; you will see that the distance between them alters. This is because the boom has to be pulled in or let out to keep the sails at a constant angle to the wind as the course and point of sailing changes.

Balance

You will have quickly learned to balance your dinghy by sitting on the side and leaning out, using your toe straps, when the craft heels. Sailing a dinghy on its side with water lapping the lower gunwale is quite exciting, but actually not very efficient. Dinghies sail faster when they are kept flat. They are also easier to steer, because when a dinghy

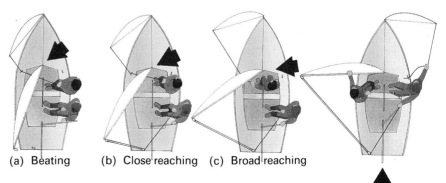

(a) Beating   (b) Close reaching   (c) Broad reaching

▲ *Fig. 25 Showing the position of the crew*

(d) Running   27

heels away from the wind it has a tendency to turn itself towards the wind. To make it behave and sail in a straight line you will need to pull hard on the tiller to compensate and this extra drag will slow you down. Fig. 25 (*see* page 27) shows the crew's position at each point during sailing.

Centreboard

The centreboard prevents the dinghy from sliding sideways through the water when the wind is blowing from the side, and particularly from the side and ahead as in beating. The closer you sail towards the wind, the greater the sideways forces and the greater the effect of the centreboard. Obviously the mere fact of pulling the centreboard through the water creates friction, and it is only reasonable to use as little of it in the water as is necessary. If you are sailing upwind, however, its function in preventing sideways slip compensates for the drag which it creates. As the dinghy sails away from the wind (the wind moving around to the side) side slip will reduce and less centreboard is

necessary. When you have sailed so far away from the wind that you are running (*see* fig. 22) then there will be no sideways drift at all and only the tip of the centreboard will be needed to help the dinghy sail more steadily in a straight line.

Trim

If you study the drawing of a dinghy, you will see that the water-line runs its full length, with the stern of the dinghy just sitting on that line. As you sail along, your boat has to push the water

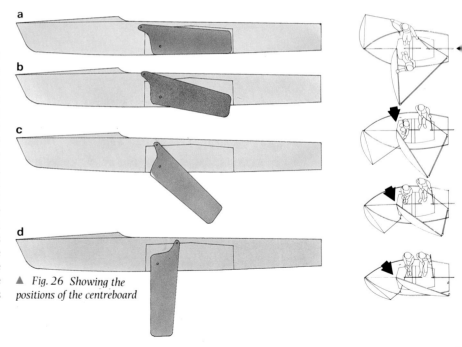

▲ *Fig. 26 Showing the positions of the centreboard*

28

out of the way; but if you sit too far to the back, so that the stern sinks below the water, then it will be pushing water to the surface in a cascade of bubbles. If your dinghy is trimmed correctly then the water should leave the stern smoothly without any fuss or commotion.

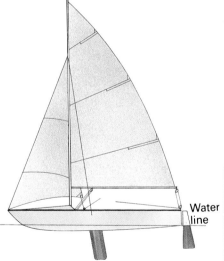

▲ Fig. 27 The water-line

Course

Where there is sufficient wind and water, a dinghy can be sailed to almost any destination. However, it is not always possible in a straight line. If you are sailing up-wind then you do so in a series of zig-zags. For someone who doesn't understand how a sailboat works, watching a fleet sail up-wind must be very confusing: no one seems to be sailing directly towards where they want to be!

When sailing up-wind you must take advantange of every change in the wind's direction. If you are beating with your sails pulled in tightly, and your mainsail and jib begin to flutter, you will need to turn your dinghy away from the wind slightly until the sails fill properly again. Unfortunately this means that you have turned a little away from the direction in which you were heading. Small alterations in course are inevitable, but if the wind changes so much that you have to turn away from your course quite dramatically then it is better to tack and sail with the wind on the other side.

▲ Fig. 28 Sailing to an upwind goal (beating)

29

Spinnakers

Many two-handed dinghies carry a third sail, called a spinnaker, to increase power down, and sometimes across, the wind.

The sail is usually symmetrical and is flown on port or starboard either ahead and to weather of the mainsail and jib (running) or ahead but on the same side as the mainsail (reaching). The head of the sail is tied to the spinnaker halyard which comes from the top of the mast above the jib sheave. The two bottom corners are tied to port and starboard sheets which are then led through blocks near the dinghy's stern and finally forward to the thwart where they can be controlled by the crew.

For the first launch the dinghy is turned onto a run so that the stowed spinnaker is on the same side as the mainsail. This will allow it to be hoisted behind the mainsail, where it will be sheltered. Once the spinnaker is hoisted fully, the crew pulls the guy to which the pole has been attached into the wind and the sail will set (fig. 30(a)–(d)).

To lower the spinnaker, the helmsman stands steering with the tiller between his knees, the pole is removed and the crew gathers up the foot of the sail and pulls it into the weather side of the dinghy as it is lowered by the helmsman.

The procedure illustrated is for a leeward hoist. To hoist from the windward side the crew must gather up the spinnaker and throw it upwards and forwards into the airstream. The pole is attached when the spinnaker is flying. The spinnaker can be gybed using the following procedure.

- First unclip the spinnaker pole from the mast and then the pole from the guy.
- The pole will still be hanging from the uphaul/downhaul.
- The helmsman will be steering with the tiller between his knees, but will also be holding the spinnaker guy and sheet to keep the sail flying.
- The crew gybes the mainsail and then re-attaches the pole to the sail and mast.

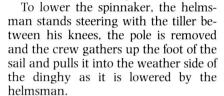

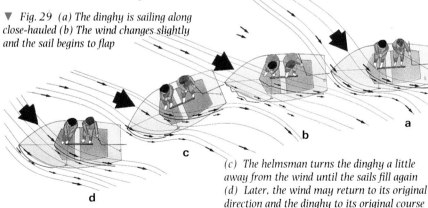

▼ *Fig. 29 (a) The dinghy is sailing along close-hauled (b) The wind changes slightly and the sail begins to flap*

(c) The helmsman turns the dinghy a little away from the wind until the sails fill again (d) Later, the wind may return to its original direction and the dinghy to its original course

You may start by sailing on a run, but it is possible to broad reach with the spinnaker. The pole will have to swing further and further forward towards the forestay as you turn to sail across the wind. Except in very light airs it will take helm and crew on the windward side to balance the dinghy. If you are over-powered, turn further away from the wind until you are running again.

Crewing

Much of this book is concerned with the job of helming a dinghy. However, successful sailing in a two-person dinghy depends on good teamwork between the helmsman and the crew. The crew manages the foresail and spinnaker (if fitted), and both sails need constant adjustment. The jib setting is critical if the helmsman is to get the best out of the mainsail. As the helmsman, your position will be more or less fixed so that you can hold the tiller extension and mainsheet to control the dinghy. Your crew will be much more mobile and will not only control the foresails but will be periodically adjusting position in order

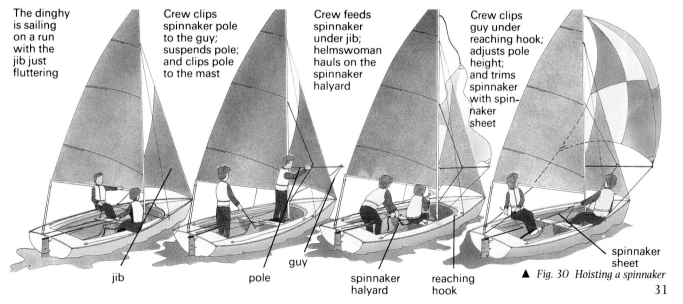

The dinghy is sailing on a run with the jib just fluttering

Crew clips spinnaker pole to the guy; suspends pole; and clips pole to the mast

Crew feeds spinnaker under jib; helmswoman hauls on the spinnaker halyard

Crew clips guy under reaching hook; adjusts pole height; and trims spinnaker with spin-naker sheet

jib

pole

guy

spinnaker halyard

reaching hook

spinnaker sheet

▲ *Fig. 30 Hoisting a spinnaker*

to balance the boat. The crew also serves as a lookout and may well be able to advise on tactics during racing. You and your crew should practise together so that your tacking and gybing are well coordinated with movement across the boat, and your sail-release and setting are in perfect harmony.

Many of the figures show the crew position at various points during sailing. Although in windy weather both members of the crew may be sitting well out on the same side, in lighter conditions this may not be necessary.

▲ *This dinghy is fitted with a trapeze so that the crew can move well out and keep the craft properly balanced*

Tides

Sailing in tidal waters needs some thought. The tidal stream in the middle of an estuary, where water is often at its deepest, flows much more quickly than it does in the shallower water nearest the shore. If you are sailing *with* the tide, it may help you along if you sail where the tide is stronger. However, since the deepest channels are used by deep-draught commercial ships, it would be unwise to sail amongst them; it is always better to sail to one side of the main channel and never actually in it.

If your destination takes you *against* the tide, you will make better way sailing nearer the shore where there may be slacker water. Often when people are planning a daysail in their dinghy, they check the tide for the day and sail with it to their destination. They then wait for the tide to turn and sail back home, using the tide to help them. This can be a very useful strategy, particularly if the wind drops!

It is worth taking time to study the effects of tide in your sailing area. The

direction can be determined from the way moored boats are pointing, buoys are leaning and the way water builds up against jetty posts and stanchions. The photograph opposite shows the strength and direction of the tide as it flows past a port channel buoy. Tide tables are usually published in small-book form for local harbours and resorts and are obtainable from chandlers and sometimes even newsagents. If there is a harbour-master, tide tables or the tidal state for each day may be posted outside on a notice board with a weather forecast. During the ebb and the flood the

▲ *A dinghy sailing outside the main shipping channel*

flow of water increases and decreases in such a way that the strongest flow is midway between high and low water. If you are staying locally and are not planning to use the tide for a day sail, it is better to sail for an hour each side of high or low water. This is especially true if there is not very much wind, since you may find otherwise that you are pushing into a current against which you cannot make progress. During the first hour $\frac{1}{12}$ of the water will flow in or out; in the second hour $\frac{2}{12}$; in the third and fourth hour $\frac{3}{12}$; $\frac{2}{12}$ in the fifth; and $\frac{1}{12}$ in the sixth hour.

▲ The strength and direction of the tide – a port channel buoy

Where to sail

Initially, all your sailing should be in safe waters – areas that are used by other dinghy sailors and where help is at hand if things go badly wrong. Always make sure that someone ashore knows that you are sailing and give them a time when you are likely to return ashore. There is no doubt that joining a sailing club has many advantages. Sailing with others is often safer: most clubs have a powered safety boat and provide a degree of supervision. Many clubs have members who are instructors.

If after a season's sailing you decide to sail in tidal waters without supervision, then you and your boat have to be prepared accordingly. If you do venture out, you need to be as self-sufficient as is reasonably possible. Make sure that you have studied the area in which you intend sailing. Make a note of the landmarks ashore which may help to guide you home again. Identify the main shipping channel, mooring areas or places of particular danger, and plan to avoid

▲ Clubs and sailing schools have safety boats

them. Check the tides: when is high tide and when is low? If you stay out too long you may have difficulty returning through lack of water! Check which way the tidal stream is running and how strong it is likely to be. Most small-boat sailors sail a couple of hours each side of high tide, before the tidal stream reaches its maximum speed. This also ensures sufficient water for their return.

Conditions on open water can change quite dramatically, so remember to dress appropriately. It is well worth while taking spare warm clothing in a sealed plastic bag. A first aid kit is useful, as is a flask or two filled with warm drinks and perhaps even some suntan lotion and sunglasses – there can be quite a strong glare from the sea and from white sails on a sunny day.

Your dinghy should be carefully checked before launching to make sure that nothing is badly worn to a point where it could let you down. It is also a good idea to have an emergency bag containing spare shackles, string and rope, insulating tape, a sharp knife, a pair of pliers and even a screwdriver, taped securely aboard.

Even windsurfers with their own tiny craft invest in a pack of mini-flares. The sets sold by most chandlers are not much larger than a postcard and take up very little space. Usually there are an equal number of red flares (used if you are in danger and distress) and white flares which indicate your position and that you require help. A big orange smoke float is a good investment if you are sailing in estuaries.

▲ *Fig. 31 An imaginary estuary*

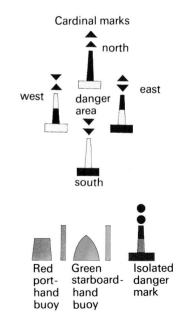

Fig. 32 Buoyage system ▶

Anchoring

Although you may well be able to slow and even stop your dinghy, it will still continue to drift in the wind and be swept along by the tide. If you need to stay in one place then the only sure way is to drop your anchor. When preparing your anchor before setting sail, make sure that you have the type which best suits the seabed conditions and will grip the bottom when needed. Make sure also that the anchor is large enough to hold the weight and windage of your dinghy, and that you have sufficient rope, or warp, to reach the bottom three or more times over. As you slowly let down your anchor, estimate the depth and then lay out the extra line. Remember, as the tide turns your dinghy will turn too, so make sure that there is plenty of room to avoid fouling any obstructions.

The anchor can be kept in a bucket and the bucket used to bail out, should the dinghy be filled with water for any reason. Most modern dinghies are now equipped with self-bailers which draw water out of the dinghy as it sails along. These work in reverse when the dinghy is stationary, so if you stop remember to close them!

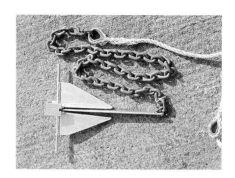

A Danforth anchor fitted with a length of ▷ *chain so that the pull, when it is under load, will be horizontal. The anchor should be tied down inside the dinghy so that it cannot slide about and cause damage*

Capsizing

A large yacht has a heavy keel to prevent it from capsizing (a toy yacht has exactly the same system). The centreboard of a sailing dinghy is usually made of wood and, compared with the weight of the dinghy, is very light. The dinghy relies on the weight of the crew to keep it upright, and part of the skill of sailing is the ability to move your weight about to maintain this balance. Inevitably mishaps occur, balance is lost and the boat capsizes. Initially the dinghy lies on its side for a short time, and it is essential that the crew drop into the water so as not to pull the dinghy over completely (fig. 33(a)). Personal buoyancy, which should always be worn while sailing, will allow you to float fairly effortlessly in the water, and you should make your way to the stern. If there is a tangle then this can be sorted out (fig. 33(b)).

The procedure for righting the boat is as follows:

● The crew stays put and the helmsman swims to the centreboard holding on to the mainsheet as a lifeline (fig. 33(c)). The crew swims between the boom and the inside of the dinghy to the centreboard case. The crew can then

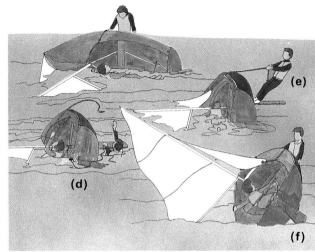

▲ *Fig. 33 Capsizing*

call through the centreboard slot and warn his partner before pushing down the centreboard fully. While the crew is in position he should hold on to the dinghy below the waterline, so as not to pull the dinghy further over.

● The crew throws the top jibsheet over to the helmsman so that it can be used to climb onto the centreboard (fig. 33(d)).

● With the crew lying alongside the centreline of the dinghy, the helmsman leans back and pulls on the jibsheet.

● Keeps his feet close to the hull and his back straight (fig. 33(e)).

● As the dingy comes upright, the crew rolls in and is then able to help the helmsman back on board (fig. 33(f)).

Sometimes the dinghy can be righted by the helmsman standing on the submerged gunwale; some lighter dinghies can be righted by simply pulling on the side.

If the dinghy does turn right over, bring it to the lay-down position described above by sinking the windward back corner to start the roll and then moving along the side to pull on the centreboard.

When the dinghy is upright it will be full of water and quite unstable until most of it has been emptied out. Before sailing away it is better to set to work with a bucket and then use the selfbailers when the dinghy is more manageable.

▲ *Righting a dinghy*

Stopping

To stop your dinghy, simply let the sails flap and you will lose power. You may drift in the tide, but on still water you will slow almost to a stop. If you want to stop for a while, perhaps to put on more clothing or to have something to eat or drink, a better way is to heave to. Sail along on port tack with the jib cleated. Leave the jib cleated and tack onto starboard, push the tiller away and completely release the mainsheet. The jib and mainsail are now working against each other and the result is stalemate! You will continue to drift (wind and tide), so keep a look out.

If you lose a crew member over the side you will need to return to him, stop and pick him up. Whoever is left in the dinghy should regain control and sail away on a beam reach. The jib can be left flapping. Keep an eye on the person in the water, tack and sail back on a beam reach. Start to bear away a little as you get closer, then turn your dinghy onto a close reach and slow down by letting out the mainsheet. If you have stopped you will be able to let go of the tiller and help your crew member in near the windward shroud. If you have not managed to stop, sail away again and repeat the manoeuvre.

Stopping a dinghy in this particular way is useful for picking up moorings and coming alongside other craft, so it is well worth practising (fig. 34).

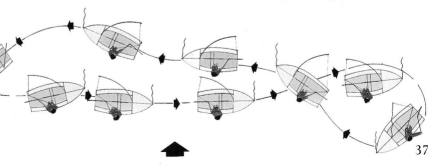

▲ *Fig. 34 Stopping (e.g. man overboard)*

Rules of the road

Having a wide stretch of water without the hazards that beset the motorist is one of the many attractions of dinghy-sailing. There are other sailors, however, and so regulations are necessary to prevent collisions.

Traditionally, powered vessels were expected to give way to those under sail, and in the days of four-masted tall ships this made perfect sense. Large powered vessels are often restricted by their own size and the depth of water beneath them, making it unreasonable to expect them to alter course for a small sailing dinghy. It is good seamanship not to sail in a shipping channel, but if you find it necessary, take the quickest route available to avoid getting in the way of larger ships.

There are, then, a few simple rules to avoid accidents between dinghies and other sailing craft:

- If you have the wind on your starboard side (your sails then to port), you have the right of way when approaching a sailing boat on the opposite tack (fig. 35).
- If you are overtaking another dinghy you should do so without getting in the way (fig. 36).
- If you are being overtaken you should hold your course.
- A dinghy to windward of another should give way (fig. 37).

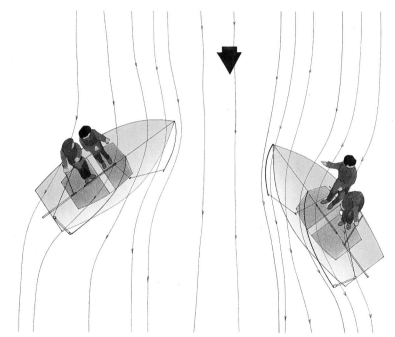

Fig. 35 The port–starboard rule ▶

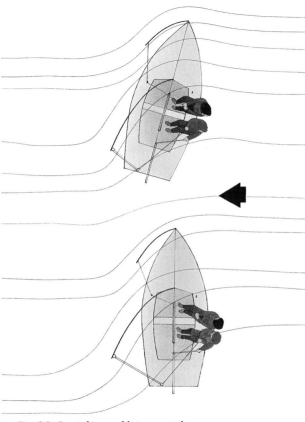

▲ Fig. 36 Overtaking and being overtaken

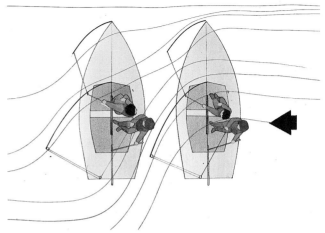

▲ Fig. 37 Windward and leeward

Racing rules

If dinghies are racing, the above rules apply, along with others that concern starting and finishing a race, tactics during the race, rounding marks and finishing. If you do decide to race, the basic rules will suffice to start with and you can add to your understanding as you become more experienced.

Racing

Cruising in a small dinghy is perfectly possible, but generally time and conditions do offer constraints. Many sailors sail on small inland ponds and lakes, and cruising is only possible during holidays. Sailing on a lake is enjoyable in itself, because wind and weather conditions are so variable and there is always something new to learn and experience. Racing is also a popular option. It allows you to measure your skill against others and to work to improve. Many sailors are reluctant to race at first, finding the closeness of other dinghies – particularly at the start – intimidating. Generally, however, the more experienced sailors will keep clear as long as you observe the basic rules.

The course

Racing is a test of boat-handling skills on every point of sailing, and the course is set with this in mind. First a start line is set across the wind with space enough for everyone to start (fig. 38). The dinghies are sailed below the line until the signals to start is made and then off they go. Sailing towards the line on starboard tack is the safest way to start and care must be taken not to sail down on to someone else (windward boat rule). In the photograph, the Enterprise dinghies have just started a race. The dinghies on port tack will have to take care to keep clear of those on starboard tack.

The next mark is placed to windward so that everyone has to beat towards it. Dinghies will be changing from starboard to port and port to starboard tacks regularly, so it is very important to know and observe the port–starboard rule (fig. 35).

The dinghy sails around the windward mark (fig. 39) – without touching

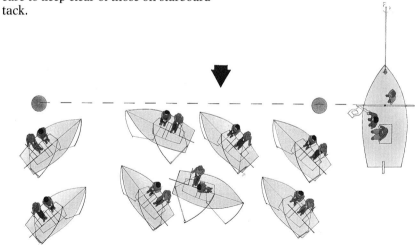

▲ *Fig. 38 Starting a race*

Fig. 39 Sailing around the triangle

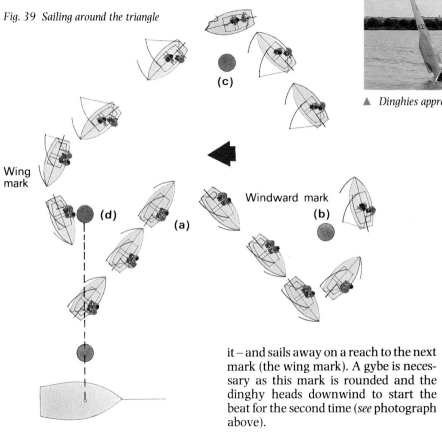

Wing mark

(d)

(c)

Windward mark

(b)

(a)

▲ *Dinghies approaching and gybing around the wing mark*

▲ *Enterprise dinghies starting a race*

it – and sails away on a reach to the next mark (the wing mark). A gybe is necessary as this mark is rounded and the dinghy heads downwind to start the beat for the second time (*see* photograph above).

The race may consist of one or several rounds of the triangular course with a final beat to the finish. To include running, the first triangle may be followed by a 'sausage'. On reaching the windward mark the dinghy ignores the wing mark and sails straight downwind to start the beat again (fig. 40). Having sailed the 'sausage' the crew sail around the triangle for the second time. After completing the triangles, or the triangle and 'sausage' course, the racers then sail a final beat to the finish.

Each racing class is allocated an International Code Flag which is hoisted ten minutes before the start of its race. Five minutes after the hoist a second flag is flown, blue and white, code flag 'P'. This warns the dinghies that the race is about to start. The two flags are dropped five minutes later, and everyone starts the race. The flags signal the stages in the starting procedure, but a sound signal is made each time a flag is hoisted or lowered to draw attention to what is happening.

If someone has started too soon the race officer may call him back, or he may be disqualified. If several dinghies have misjudged the start and are over the line, the race officer may sound two signals, hoist flag code 'general substitute', and call everyone back to restart the race.

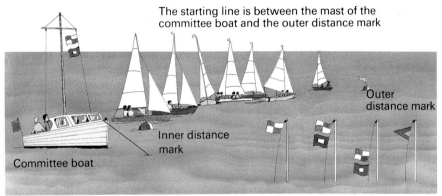

The starting line is between the mast of the committee boat and the outer distance mark

Outer distance mark

Inner distance mark

Committee boat

| Class flag – hoisted 10 minutes before start of race | Blue Peter – hoisted 5 minutes before start of race | Both flags lowered – race starts | Genera recall – the rac will be restarte |

▲ Fig. 40 Sailing a 'sausage'

▲ Fig. 41 Flags

Leaving and returning to shore

Although collisions at sea are possible, more damage is done to dinghies while leaving or returning to the shore. Coming ashore too quickly, and allowing the dinghy to touch bottom on stony shores, are common problems; once the dinghy is in deep water it is generally safe from impact damage.

To leave shore the dinghy has to be turned so that it is sideways to the wind before the crew joins the helmsman aboard. This means that when they are both aboard the dinghy can be sailed into deeper water. If the wind is blowing parallel to the shore then this is easy enough. If the wind is offshore the dinghy has to be turned away through 180°. The procedure is much the same as above, but it may help to back the jib (fig. 42).

Launching with the wind blowing onshore is more difficult; the dinghy cannot be sailed directly into the wind, and it is difficult to sail across the wind

▲ *Fig. 42 Leaving with the wind blowing offshore*

in shallow water where there is insufficient depth to push down the centreboard. If the beach shelves fairly quickly the dinghy can be sailed on the best tack (the one that points the dinghy further away from the shore) and the crew can gradually lower the centreboard as the dinghy sails into deeper water (fig. 43).

If this is not possible then paddling a little way out is the answer. Coming ashore with the wind blowing onshore makes a controlled landing difficult because it is not easy to depower the sails on a run. The answer is to approach the shore, turn into the wind and drop the mainsail, and then run ashore under jib alone. When making the approach, the crew should make sure that the main halyard is not tangled so that it doesn't jam as the sail is dropped (fig. 44).

With the wind offshore or parallel to the shore, the dinghy can be sailed into knee-deep water then turned into the wind. As the turn is completed the crew jumps out to hold the dinghy head to wind while the sails are lowered.

▲ *Fig. 43 Leaving with an onshore wind*

▲ *Fig. 44 Coming ashore with the wind blowing onshore*

Choosing a dinghy

Second-hand dinghies are advertised in the yachting press, national and local newspapers and specialist magazines. Before making a purchase it is worth while conducting a bit of research. First of all, where will you sail your dinghy? Find out the location of all your local sailing clubs and pay each a visit. Depending on the size and location of the water, clubs will favour certain dinghy classes. Generally, sailing clubs favour 'one of a kind' races, aimed to encourage as few class types as possible. Usually there is a medium-sized two-person boat, a junior dinghy and perhaps a class of single-handers. Depending on your own circumstances you may be able to make a choice that suits what you want to do – racing, cruising, family sailing, single-handed sailing. Talk to other club members, as they will probably know of suitable dinghies that are for sale. If you do buy a dinghy which is popular at your local club then the chances are that its popularity may help to maintain its value, which is useful if you decide to sell it again. Most newcomers to the sport show no interest in racing and predict that they never will, but buying a popular dinghy keeps your options open for later.

New craft are always an option and there are still many builders making beautifully constructed dinghies. Again, sailing club secretaries and club fleet captains may well put you in touch with current builders. Building from a prepared kit is a good way of saving money and is quite within the scope of the average do-it-yourself householder. The high level of accurate machining that now goes into kit preparation means that kit boats go together with great simplicity. A further option is to complete a dinghy that is only part-built: usually the hull is complete and the owner then decks the boat and fits it out.

Glass-fibre hulls are popular for boats offered complete or ready for fitting out. Plywood is the favoured material for complete kit boats. Both materials have advantages and disadvantages. Plywood can be flat-packed for easy transport and is easily worked. The finished craft will need its coatings of paint and

▲ *The Laser dinghy has a wide following and is very popular for racing. This high-performance dinghy takes a little time to master*

varnish conscientiously maintained, and must be well covered and protected from the elements when not in use. Glass-fibre construction is not really a practical proposition for the amateur builder, as it requires moulds and materials that are difficult to work. Glass-fibre hulls may be thought less attractive than plywood ones, but in the long term the material is far more durable and requires very little maintenance.

▲ The Optimist dinghy is very popular throughout the world. A very safe and suitable dinghy for children from the age of eight to twelve years

▲ Enterprise dinghies racing. The Enterprise is a very popular dinghy class

▽ The 420 is a fast three-sail dingy (mainsail, jib and spinnaker) which is popular with tennagers and lighter adults

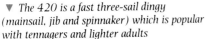

▲ The Wayfarer is a large dinghy ideal for cruising. The Wayfarer is the popular choice of many sailing schools

▲ The Topper dinghy has a wide appeal as a simple, very portable single-hander

▽ Children enjoying Mirror sailing. Many families own and sail Mirrors: they can be purchased ready-built or in easy-to-assemble kit form

▲ A group of school Wayfarers lying on moorings at a sailing school in Turkey

▲ The Sunbird has a weighted daggerboard and the sailor does not have to sit on the side to balance it. This dinghy is proving popular for people who have limited mobility

▽ The Laser II is a light, fast dinghy with trapeze and spinnaker (Cobh)

Knots

Learning to tie proper knots (as opposed to 'granny' knots) has two main advantages. The most important is that a good knot, correctly tied and designed for the job, is less likely to come undone. The other advantage is that, when you want to undo a knot, a proper one can be untied more easily. Learning to tie knots is great fun, a very useful small-boat skill and a hobby in itself. Try the ones illustrated. If you get the bug then there are specialist books available.

Used to secure a dinghy

▲ *Fig. 45 Round turn and two half hitches*

General purpose

▲ *Fig. 46 Reef knot*

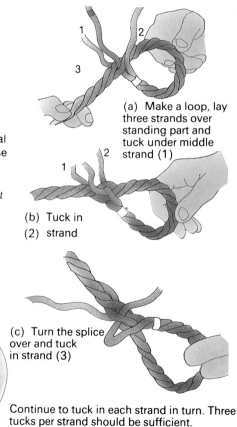

(a) Make a loop, lay three strands over standing part and tuck under middle strand (1)

(b) Tuck in (2) strand

(c) Turn the splice over and tuck in strand (3)

Continue to tuck in each strand in turn. Three tucks per strand should be sufficient.

▲ *Fig. 51 An eye splice*

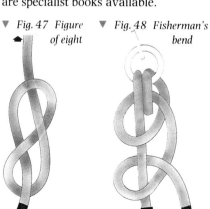

▼ *Fig. 47 Figure of eight*

▼ *Fig. 48 Fisherman's bend*

Stopper knot

Tying a line to an anchor

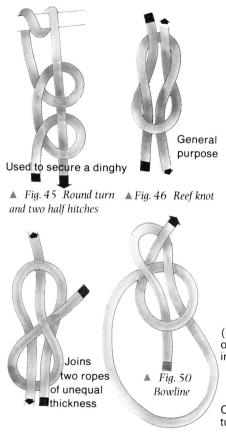

Joins two ropes of unequal thickness

▲ *Fig. 50 Bowline*

▲ *Fig. 49 Sheet bend*

47

Index